MW01675331

Vegetarian

Nita Mehta's

51 Recipes for controlling Diabetes

Nita Mehta

B.Sc. (Home Science), M.Sc. (Food and Nutrition), Gold Medalist

Co-author

RAJSHRI

(*Dietetics & Public Health Nutrition, Lady Irwin College*)

SNAB

Excellence in Books

Nita Mehta's
51 Recipes for controlling Diabetes

© Copyright 2009 SNAB Publishers Pvt Ltd

WORLD RIGHTS RESERVED. The contents—all recipes, photographs and drawings are original and copyrighted. No portion of this book shall be reproduced, stored in a retrieval system or transmitted by any means, electronic, mechanical, photocopying, recording or otherwise, without the written permission of the publishers.

While every precaution is taken in the preparation of this book, the publisher and the author assume no responsibility for errors or omissions. Neither is any liability assumed for damages resulting from the use of information contained herein.

TRADEMARKS ACKNOWLEDGED. Trademarks used, if any, are acknowledged as trademarks of their respective owners. These are used as reference only and no trademark infringement is intended upon.

First Edition 2009

ISBN 978-81-7869-276-0

Food Styling and Photography: SNAB

Layout and Laser Typesetting :

N.I.T.A. ☎ 23252948
National Information Technology Academy
3A/3, Asaf Ali Road
New Delhi-110002

Published by :

SNAB Excellence in Books
Publishers Pvt. Ltd.
3A/3 Asaf Ali Road,
New Delhi - 110002
Tel: 23252948, 23250091
Telefax:91-11-23250091

Editorial and Marketing office:
E-159, Greater Kailash-II, N.Delhi-48
Fax:91-11-29225218, 29229558
Tel:91-11-29214011, 29218574
E-Mail: nitamehta@email.com
nitamehta@nitamehta.com
Website:http://www.nitamehta.com
Website: http://www.snabindia.com

Contributing Writers :
Anurag Mehta
Subhash Mehta

Editorial & Proofreading :
Rakesh
Ramesh

Distributed by :

THE VARIETY BOOK DEPOT
A.V.G. Bhavan, M 3 Con Circus,
New Delhi - 110 001
Tel : 23417175, 23412567; Fax : 23415335
Email: varietybookdepot@rediffmail.com

Printed by :

CANARA TRADERS & PRINTERS PVT. LTD.,
CHENNAI.

Rs. 125/-

Introduction

Diabetes is a lifestyle disease. Millions of diabetics live a long, healthy life by taking care of their day-to-day health, and so can you!

Diabetes thrives on obesity and physical inactivity. A healthy, well balanced diet with good food combinations will keep diabetes under control. The recipes have been specially created using vegetables, fruits, pulses and cereals, which help in keeping the blood sugar under control. Several recipes of fenugreek (*methi*), bitter gourd (*karela*), guava (*amrood*) and *jamun* - all good foods for diabetes will add variety and flavour in a diabetic meal. The recipes are low in calories and great in taste. The herbs and spices, which are good for a diabetic, are used in the recipes to enhance taste. Enjoy life to the hilt!

Nita Mehta

Contents

Introduction 3
Understanding Diabetes 6
What is a Diabetic Diet? 9
Food Groups & Diabetes 11
Include these in a Diabetic Diet 15

Breakfast & Tea Time Snacks 20

Mushroom and Tomato Snack 21
Assorted Idlis 22
Oat Veggie Uthapam 24
Baked Lentil Squares 26
Spicy Vegetable Dalia 28
Grilled Tulsi Paneer 30
Grilled Roundels 32
Hare Kebabs 34
Mushroom Rolls 36
Pita Wraps 38

Salads & Soups 41

Stir Fried Salad 42
Cucumber Cold Soup 45
Spinach Orange Salad 46
Chinese Vegetable Soup 48

Vegetables & Dals 50

Guava Subzi 51
Stuffed Karela 52
Oregano Tindas 55
Motiya Karela 56
Mint Nugget Casserole 58
Cabbage with Peas 60
Jhatpat Kaddu 62
Lauki aur Matar Milan 64
Methi Amrood ki Subzi 67
Achaari Broccoli & Pumpkin 70
Baked Spinach Paneer 72
Baked Broccoli 75

WHAT'S IN A CUP?

INDIAN CUP
1 teacup = 200 ml liquid
AMERICAN CUP
1 cup = 240 ml liquid (8 oz.)
The recipes in this book were tested with the Indian teacup which holds 200 ml liquid.

Ajwaini Phalli 76
Mix Vegetable Saag 78
Achaari Amla Subzi 80
Sweet and Sour Karelas 81
Grilled Masala Gobhi 82
Tulsi Tori Paneer 84
Stuffed Tinda 86
Moong Dal with Carrot & Beans ... 88
Lauki in Tomato Gravy 90
Dal Medley 92

Rotis & Rice 94

Karela Roti 95
Kasoori Roti 96
Oat Bran Mooli Roti 97
Missi Mooli ki Roti 98
Spiced Paalak Roti 99
Nugget Pulao 100

Raitas, Pickles & Chutneys 103

Jamun Chutney 104
Guava Raita 105
Amla Pickle 106

Sweet Dishes 108

Stewed Guava Cups 109
Lauki & Carrot Kheer 112
Pineapple Sandesh 114
Chenna Kulfi 116
Mocha Chocolate Mousse 118
Almond Panna Cotta 120

Glossary of Names/Terms 123
International Conversion Guide . 124

Understanding Diabetes

What is Diabetes?

Food that we eat is converted to glucose which is then broken down to give energy. In a diabetic patient, the glucose cannot be digested or broken down and hence cannot be absorbed by the cells of the body. It remains in the blood thus raising the blood sugar/glucose level. When the blood sugar level rises, the body does its best to get rid of some of the extra glucose and hence some glucose is thrown out of the body through urine, which is why the glucose level in the urine also rises.

Pancreases are responsible for utilizing the glucose efficiently. This is because they secrete the hormone insulin, which helps our tissues to absorb the glucose from our blood so that the cells can use it for producing energy. When the pancrease do not produce enough insulin or the body cannot use the insulin that is produced to metabolize glucose, glucose remains in the blood and there is a rise in blood glucose level.

Causes...

- Genetic factors - If one of your parents is a diabetic, your chances of being one by the time you turn 40, are 40%.

- Obesity is a great risk factor for diabetes. Omentum fat (belly fat) contributes to diabetes by making it difficult to get glucose inside the cell & let insulin do what it does best: deliver glucose to the cells for absorption. Simply being over weight, especially having a waist greater then 37" for women and 40" for men, makes your body less sensitive to insulin, leaving the glucose to float around in your blood.

  Omentum fat is also selfish, it uses up the insulin so it can't do its job. One study shows omentum fat sucks up a quarter of the insulin that passes through the blood supply.

- Other factors which may provoke diabetes are stressful life style, high B.P., history of gestational diabetes (diabetes during pregnancy) and use of certain drugs like oral contraceptives.

Desirable Blood Glucose Levels

Fasting	:	80-110 mg/dl
Pre-meal	:	Less than 130 mg/dl
Post Meal (PP)	:	Less than 140 mg/dl

A diabetic should strive to maintain blood sugar level as close to normal level as possible.

What if Diabetes is not Kept Under Control?

Excessive glucose in the blood causes narrowing of the arteries (atherosclerosis). When it affects the larger blood vessels it results in cardiovascular problems like strokes and angina. When it affects the smaller blood vessels like capillaries in the eyes, it results in the vision-impairment caused by damage to the retina and can even cause blindness. It also leads to the inflammation of the nerve sheaths, which results in sensations like pins and needles, numbness, cramps and in severe cases, even gangrene.

Does Diabetes Ever Go Away?

No. It can always be controlled with diet and exercise and one should feel completely well. Even when treated, however, it must still be carefully watched and regularly checked for the rest of your life.

Managing Diabetes...

Although type II diabetes cannot be cured, it can be controlled and managed through regular monitoring, healthy eating and exercise. You need to understand how to manage your life style with the disease so that you can prevent yourself from the other severe problems mentioned above. Regular exercise and a well-balanced, nutritionally sound diet within permissible limits can maintain and control blood glucose levels close to normal levels, resulting in a feeling of well-being and satisfaction, ideal weight and delays the onset of complications linked with diabetes.

What is a Diabetic Diet?

A sound diabetic menu plan will let you eat normal tasty food of your choice, with the exception of foods containing added sugar, jaggery and honey, and food with excessive fats. The diet of the diabetic should be as similar to the family diet as possible. In general you will probably follow the same diet recommended by nutritionists for everybody - one that is low in fat and sugar, high in whole grains, fruits and vegetables, moderate in protein and little or no alcohol.

1. Include more fruit, vegetables and whole meal bread in you diet, which will boost the amount of fibre you eat. Fibre is now considered to be very helpful in controlling diabetes and possibly avoiding some of its complications. Do include tofu, soya nuggets, barley, gelatine, papaya, melon, grape fruit, guava, amla, jamuns and oranges in your diet.

2. Avoid all sugar and sugar containing foods (e.g. sweets, chocolates, cakes, pudding, sweet biscuits, squashes, fizzy drinks and fruit tinned in syrup).

3. Eat regularly. It is important not to miss meals as this can cause your blood sugar levels to vary too much. Aim to eat three times a day, with a drink and a biscuit or a piece of fruit in between.

4. Try to avoid fatty foods. This applies to all diabetics, whether overweight or not. Follow these tips to reduce fat in your diet ...

   - Use a non stick *kadhai* for cooking food.
   - Always use a spoon to measure oil. Never pour oil into the *kadhai* or pan.
   - Cut vegetables into big chunks. They absorb less oil.
   - Eat home made cottage cheese (*paneer*) and yogurt (*dahi*) prepared from toned milk.
   - Remember that cakes, pastries, sauces etc. are all fatty – even though you can't see it.
   - Particularly try to avoid animal fats like butter/ghee. These saturated fats can increase the risk of coronary heart disease in diabetes.
   - Eat eggs only three times a week and eat only small amounts of cheddar and similar cheeses. Eat only lean meat or poultry.

Food Groups & Diabetes

Carbohydrates

Earlier it was presumed that diabetes is a carbohydrate intolerance disease. But now it is recommended to have a high fibre carbohydrate diet for diabetics. 45% to 50% calories consumed should be from carbohydrates.

For a diabetic person it is important to know how much and what kind of carbohydrate is eaten in a meal. Carbohydrates are the first to get converted into glucose. There are some carbohydrates which instantly get converted to glucose and suddenly raise the blood sugar level. These are **bad carbohydrates** and include sugars and refined cereals like *maida* and white bread and polished white rice. Since refined foods contain no fibre which means the calories are released easily and blood sugar level rises swiftly, excess intake of refined carbohydrates can cause diabetes. But there are **good carbohydrates** too which are absorbed slowly into the blood stream and slowly get converted to glucose and give rise to a gradual rise in blood sugar levels, making it easier for the diabetics to adjust to the changes in blood glucose levels. **Good carbohydrates** are rich in fibre and include whole grain cereals like whole wheat flour (*atta*), wheat porridge (*dalia*), oats, pulses, beans, peas and unpolished or brown rice. Fruits and vegetables with the exception of a few are in general good carbohydrates. Fibre is very essential for a diabetic. Use of soluble fibre in the form of barley, oatmeal, fruits; dried beans help considerably in reducing blood sugar levels. Thus such food should be increased in the diet.

Besides the bad carbohydrates like table sugar and refined cereals, there are other foods which raise the blood sugar levels. These foods are the ones with a **"high glycemic index"**. High glycemic foods raise the glucose level in the blood instantly and hence should be avoided by the diabetics. Potato, arbi and yam are high glycemic index vegetables.

Proteins

Proteins build muscles in the body. Proteins also help in the formation of enzymes and growth of the body. 1 gm of protein provides 4 calories. Proteins are important in regulation of osmotic pressure and maintenance of body's water balance.

Proteins can be obtained from vegetable sources as well as animal sources. **Animal sources are complete proteins** whereas proteins from **plant sources** need to be **combined together to make a complete protein**. The exception is soya beans which is a complete vegetable protein with all the essential amino acids. The most important source of protein for a vegetarian is a cereal combined with a pulse. A deficiency of the protein of cereal is made up by the protein of the pulse, making the combination a complete protein, as dal-chawal (*khichri*) or rajmah-chawal. But for the vegetarians, milk and *paneer* are complete proteins.

Plant Proteins: legumes, pulses, soyabean, peanuts and other nuts.

Animal Proteins: milk, milk products as yogurt & cheese, egg, meats, fish, poultry

Fats

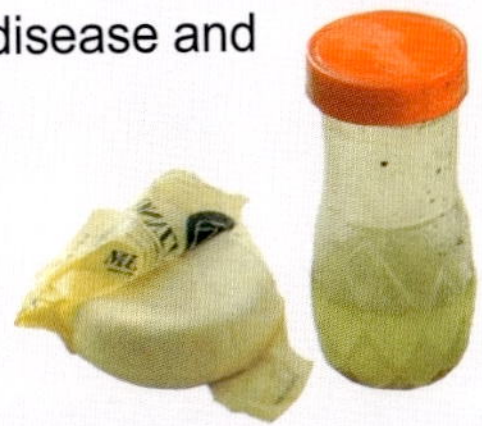

All fats and edible oils are not bad for health. While bad fats raise the risk of heart disease and diabetes, good fats protect against them.

However, excess fat prevents insulin from working properly. Too much fats in the food taxes the pancreas & hence the production of insulin is affected. Excess use of saturated fats (butter, ghee, cream) can further aggravate the situation.

Replace full cream milk and curd with toned milk and curd prepared at home with toned milk. Eat only the egg white, as the egg yolk is rich in fat. Avoid commercially prepared bakery products which are rich in transfats, which are the worst type of fats.

Approx. % of Fatty Acids in Different Cooking Mediums

Type of Fat	% of Saturated	% of Mono-Unsaturated	% of Poly-Unsaturated
Olive	13	72	08
Mustard	07	58	29
Safflower	09	12	74
Sunflower	10	20	66
Soyabean	16	44	37
Peanut	17	49	32
Coconut	87	06	02
Dalda	39	44	11
Butter	60	26	05

A healthy oil is one which has no trans fatty acids, is low in saturated fatty acids, high in mono-unsaturated fatty acids and also has same amounts of poly unsaturated fatty acids. **Olive oil & mustard oil are recommended** as they are good sources of omega 3 fatty acids, the essential poly-unsaturated fatty acids. Keep changing the cooking oil every 3 months or use a combination of 3-4 oils to get the health benefits of all of them.

Include these in a Diabetic Diet

Bitter Gourd (*Karela*)

Many shrink away from consuming *karela* because of its bitter taste, but ayurvedic experts call it a wonder drug. Include it liberally in the diabetic diet. *Karela* helps in achieving positive sugar levels by suppressing the urge for sweet taste. Rich in iron, *karela* has twice the beta carotene of broccoli, twice the calcium of spinach, twice the potassium of bananas, and contains vitamins C and B 1 to 3, phosphorous and good dietary fibre.

The juice extracted from *karela* is given to patients suffering from diabetes. In addition to preventing weight gain, extracts of unripe *karela* appear to down–regulate insulin. Several of its compounds have been confirmed to lower blood sugar, and it appears to have fewer side effects than insulin.

Cinnamon (*Dalchini)*

In a study published in Diabetes Care in 2003, researches found that an intake of 1, 3 or 6 grams of cinnamon a day reduced levels of serum glucose, LDL cholesterol, and total cholesterol in people with type 2 diabetes.

Fenugreek (*Methi*)

Commonly used in traditional Indian medicine, fenugreek has been shown to stabilize levels of glucose.

It can be taken in the form of dry fenugreek leaves (*kasoori methi*) or when in season, fresh fenugreek (*methi*) leaves can be cooked with vegetables.

1 tsp of *methi seeds* should be soaked at night in a glass of water and the water had first thing in the morning. Also the seeds can be dry roasted, and ground to powder. ½ tsp of this powder can be taken in the morning.

Soya Beans

Soya beans help in lowering the urinary sugar. Soya lecithin helps in preventing the neurological complications of diabetes. Rich in proteins, calcium and zinc. Can be taken in the form of whole soya beans or sprouts. 1 part of soya bean flour can be mixed with 4 parts of regular whole wheat flour and used for normal chappatis. Soya bean oil is also beneficial to health.

Basil (*Tulsi*)

A wonder herb. Add to vegetables or snacks instead of fresh coriander to enhance taste and food value. 5 *tulsi* leaves along with 5 pepper corns *(kali mirch)* on an empty stomach is good for diabetes.

Guava (*Amrood*)

Guava is good for diabetes. Rich in iron and vitamin C which help in digestion and is an anti-oxidant. Combine with vegetables like *methi* to make an amazing dish.

Oats

Rich in soluble fibre which is good for diabetes. Oat fibre regulates sugar metabolism. Keeps bowls clear and regulated. Porridge is not the only way to use this healthy cereal. Powder it and add to dosa or vada or idli batter. Mix oat bran with flour for making healthy chappatis. Sprinkle on fruits and bake for a healthy dessert.

Brown Rice

Brown rice is a complete food as far as nutrients are concerned. It has lots of fibre. Combine rice with lots of vegetables to reduce the quantity of carbohydrate in the diet.

Jambul Fruit (*Jamun*)

This fruit reduces blood sugar & is very good to control diabetes. Even its seed is very useful, infact it is more beneficial. Its seeds contain a glucose, jamboline which restricts the conversion of starch into sugar which helps to control diabetes. Convert jamuns into chutney and sherbet, the recipes of which are given at the end.

Channa Dal or Gram flour (*Besan*)

It utilizes the sugar in the body and thus the intake of insulin is also reduced. It also helps in muscle building and reduces the weakness in the body. Add to vegetables like *karela* or stuff cooked dal in some vegetables like *tindas* or *parwals.*

Amla

It helps to reduce the blood sugar level. Rich in vitamin C. It also helps as digestive and helps in the free flow of urine if there is any obstruction. You can mix 1 tbsp of amla juice in a cup of carrot or lauki juice.

Onion-Garlic

Helps to maintain blood sugar level. Helps as diuretic and antiseptic also. Garlic is rich in potassium. Potassium intake invigorates pancrease.

Almonds

Almonds are rich in dietary fibre, which helps to counter heart disease, diabetes, constipation & cancer. Almonds are good source of phosphorus & copper which helps to circulate oxygen to blood vessels.

Chromium & Zinc

Chromium & zinc have a positive effect on insulin signalling, leading to glucose uptake. Their deficiency has been suggested to play a role in the development of diabetes. Zinc is involved in virtually all aspects of insulin metabolism: synthesis, secretion and utilization. Soya beans are rich in zinc. It is confirmed that chromium enhances insulin production by the body and helps to stabilize blood sugar. Whole grain cereals, mushrooms, corn oil and brewer's yeast are relatively good sources of chromium.

Fibre

Increase fibre intake by adding wheat bran and green veggies (especially broccoli, beans, peas) to your diet. Fibre binds carbs and slows down food assimilation, thus averting a sudden rise in blood sugar levels. Have lots of whole grain cereals, like whole wheat flour and brown rice. Take more of whole lentils *(saboot or chilka waali dals)* which are richer in fibre as compared to *dhuli* dals. Soluble fibre present in barley, oats and fruits helps even further to lower blood sugar. Prefer fruits to fruit juices.

Breakfast & Tea Time Snacks

Mushroom and Tomato Snack

Wheat toasts topped with sliced mushrooms. Makes a perfect breakfast.

Makes 10

200 gms fresh mushrooms - thinly sliced

2-3 garlic cloves - crushed, 1 onion - thinly sliced, 2 tomatoes - chopped

1 green chilli - chopped, 1 tbsp chopped coriander, a pinch of red chilli powder

2 tsp oil

4 whole wheat bread slices - toasted, ¾ tsp salt, or to taste

HEALTH BENEFIT

Tomatoes are good for diabetes. They have a good effect on the level of urine sugar.

1. Heat the oil and stir fry the garlic and onions for 1 minute.
2. Add the tomatoes and stir again for a minute.
3. Add the green chilli, coriander and chilli powder. Stir for ½ minute.
4. Add the mushrooms and salt. Cook for 3-4 minutes. Remove from heat.
5. Cut each toasted bread slice into two. Spread the mixture on top. Serve hot.

Assorted Idlis

Vegetable puree makes these steamed cakes healthier.

Makes 12

1 cup semolina (*suji*) - roasted in 1 tsp oil for 2 minutes, 1 cup yogurt

¼ cup chopped spinach - pureed roughly in a small grinder using 1-2 tbsp water

3 tbsp ready made tomato puree, 1 tsp finely grated ginger, 1 tsp salt, 2 tsp eno fruit salt

1. Soak the semolina in curd. Add ginger. Mix well. Keep aside for 15-20 minutes till semolina turns soft. Do not keep longer. Keep 1 cup water in a deep pan with a well fitting lid on fire. See that the pan is big enough to hold the idli stand.
2. To the semolina mixture, add salt and eno. Divide the mixture into two parts. To one part, add spinach puree and to the other half add tomato puree.
3. Immediately put the batter in greased cups of the idli stand. Put the stand in the pan of boiling water. Cover pan and steam the idlis for 8-10 minutes. Shut off the fire but let the idlis be as it is in steam for 5 minutes. Remove idlis from the cups after another 5 minutes. Serve.

Oat Veggie Uthapam

These thick South Indian pancakes can be prepared without having to wait for the batter to ferment. The eno take care of the lightness without fermentation.

Makes 3-4

BATTER

1 cup oats, ½ cup semolina (*suji*), ½-¾ cup water

½ tsp salt, ¼ tsp asafoetida (*hing*) powder, ¼ tsp eno fruit salt

TOPPING

½ cup grated *paneer*, 1-2 green chillies - chopped, a few curry leaves - chopped

1 onion - chopped, 1 tomato - chopped, ¼ cup peas - boiled, ¼ cup cabbage - chopped

¼ tsp black pepper powder, salt to taste

1. Except eno mix all ingredients of the batter together.
2. Add enough water (½-¾ cup approx.) to the batter to get a thick pouring consistency. Beat well. Keep the batter aside for ½ hour. Mash well to get a binding batter.

3. At the time of preparing uthapam, add eno and mix well.

4. Mix all ingredients of the topping together. Keep aside.

5. Heat a non stick *tawa*. Put 1 tbsp of oil on it and then wipe with a potato or onion cut into half.

6. Mix the batter well. Keeping the gas on low flame, pour 1 small *karchhi* (2 tbsp) of batter on it. Spread the batter a little with the back of the *karchhi*, keeping it slightly thick.

7. Sprinkle a little topping on each and pour 2 tsp oil on the sides. Press the topping a little with a potato masher or spoon. Keep on low heat for a minute. After the edges turn golden and the underside is cooked, turn the side carefully.

8. Remove from *tawa* after the other side also gets cooked and the onions turn a little brown. Serve hot.

Baked Lentil Squares

Enjoy as a snack or put in a curry to make a baked kofta curry!

Makes 16 pieces

1 cup gram lentils (*channa dal*), 200 gm bottle gourd (*lauki*) or carrots - grated (2 cups)

1 onion - finely chopped, 2-3 green chillies - finely chopped

½ cup chopped coriander leaves, 1 tsp salt

½ tsp baking soda (*mitha soda*), 1 tsp *chaat masala*, to sprinkle

1. Soak gram lentils in water for 2-3 hours. Drain and grind to paste.
2. Mix all the ingredients, except chaat masala with the dal paste.
3. Let it stand for 10 minutes
4. Grease a baking tray and transfer the mixture in it. Shape into a square of ¼" thickness.
5. Bake in a preheated oven at 200°C, for about 15-20 minutes till top is golden brown. (approx. 15 minutes). Cut into 1" squares and serve sprinkled with *chaat masala*.

HEALTH BENEFIT

Bengal gram helps in better utilization of insulin and thus reduces the intake of insulin.

Spicy Vegetable Dalia

A fibre rich breakfast prepared from cracked wheat!

Serves 4

1 cup cracked wheat (*dalia*)

½ cup finely chopped beans, ½ cup finely chopped carrot, ½ cup finely chopped capsicum

2 tsp olive oil

1 tsp cumin seeds (*jeera*), ½ tsp fenugreek seeds (*methi dana*)

1-2 green chillies - chopped, 3 cloves garlic - chopped, 1 onion - finely chopped

¼ tsp turmeric (*haldi*), ¼ tsp red chilli powder, ½ tsp coriander (*dhania*) powder

1 tsp mint (*pudina*), 2-3 tbsp chopped coriander, 1 tsp salt, 1 tbsp lemon juice

1. Roast cracked wheat with 1 tsp oil in a non-stick pan for 7-8 minutes, on medium heat stirring constantly till it changes colour and turns fragrant. Remove from pan and keep aside.
2. Heat 1 tsp oil again in the pan. Add cumin seeds and fenugreek seeds. Wait till fenugreek seeds turn light brown.

3. Add garlic and green chillies. Stir and add onions. Stir fry on medium heat till onions turn light brown.

4. Add the cut vegetables and sauté for 3-4 minutes. Add turmeric, red chilli, coriander and salt. Mix well for 2 minutes. Cook covered for 2-3 minutes till vegetables are almost tender.

5. Add 1½ cups water, cracked wheat, mint and ½ tsp salt. Cook covered for about 10 minutes on low heat till vegetables are done and water is absorbed, stirring once or twice in between. Remove from fire. Add coriander and lemon juice. Mix and serve hot.

HEALTH BENEFIT

Fibre binds carbs & slows down the food assimilation, thus averting a sudden rise in the blood sugar levels.

Grilled Tulsi Paneer

Cottage cheese in a marinade which is herbed with fresh basil.

Makes 8 pieces

200 gms *paneer* - cut into big triangles of ½" thickness

¼ cup yogurt - hang for 30 minutes in a muslin cloth

1 tbsp gram flour (*besan*) - roasted on a *tawa* on low heat till fragrant

2 flakes garlic - crushed, 1 tsp salt, 1 tsp *chaat masala*, ¼ cup chopped basil (*tulsi*) leaves

1. Cut the *paneer* into ½" thick slices. Cut a slice diagonally to get 2 triangles. Pat dry on a clean kitchen towel to absorb any moisture present.
2. Mix the hung yogurt, roasted gram flour, garlic cloves, salt, *chaat masala* and basil. Spread the yogurt paste on both sides of the *paneer*. Keep aside for ½ to 1 hour.
3. To serve, cover a wire rack with foil and brush foil with few drops of oil. Place the *paneer* pieces on it and grill the *paneer* pieces till golden brown. Alternately, you can pan fry the *paneer* in 1 tsp oil instead of using the oven. Serve.

HEALTH BENEFIT

Tulsi is a wonder herb. Regular consumption of a few tulsi leaves, first thing in the morning can keep you healthy & disease free.

Grilled Roundels

Thick slices of grilled gourd can be used as snack or a side dish.

Serves 6

250 gm (½ of a medium *lauki*) bottle gourd (*lauki*)

¾ tsp salt

1 tbsp oil

2-3 tbsp fresh crumbs prepared by grinding a slice of whole wheat bread in a mixer

4 tsp roasted channa flour (grind roasted channas to a powder in a mixer)

2 tsp yogurt

½ tsp *chaat masala* to sprinkle

1. Peel and cut gourd into 1" round slices.
2. In a pan or *kadhai* heat 1 tbsp oil, sauté gourd rounds with salt for 3-4 minutes till gourd softens. Cover for a minute if you like it soft. Cook till dry. Remove from pan to a bowl.
3. Sprinkle bread crumbs, channa powder and curd on the gourd. Mix well so that the gourd is coated.
4. Place on a greased grill rack and grill the gourd for about 5-7 minutes till it turns golden brown.
5. Sprinkle *chaat masala* and serve hot.

HEALTH BENEFIT

Lauki is rich in vitamins & minerals. Light for the stomach and helps fight high blood pressure and obesity.

Hare Kebabs

Makes 8

2 cups finely chopped spinach leaves, ½ cup peas - boiled

½ cup crumbled home made *paneer*

1 tsp finely grated ginger

6 tbsp roasted channa powder (grind roasted channas in a mixer)

¾ tsp salt

1 tsp *channa masala*

¼ tsp *amchoor*

2 tsp oil

2 tbsp fresh bread crumbs

1. Boil 3 cups water with ½ tsp salt. Add spinach and boil for 2-3 minutes. Strain and squeeze the spinach.

2. Mix spinach, peas, *paneer* and ginger in a blender and blend coarsely.

3. Add roasted *channa* flour, salt, *channa masala* and *amchoor* to the ground mixture.

4. Grind 1 slice of brown bread to get fresh crumbs. Add 2 tbsp crumbs to the spinach mixture.

5. Make balls and flatten to form kebabs. Grease a non-stick pan with a little oil. Cook the kebabs on both sides in the pan till brown. Press lightly while they turn brown on the pan. Serve with pudina chutney.

Mushroom Rolls

A quick bite of creamy mushrooms wrapped in bread!

Makes 8

200 gms mushrooms - chopped finely

2 tsp chopped parsley or mint (*pudina*)

2 tsp cornflour

½ cup milk

1 green chilli - deseeded and chopped

½ tsp salt, ¼ tsp pepper

1 tsp lime juice

2 tsp oil

8 slices brown bread

1. Wash mushrooms and finely chop them.
2. Heat oil, sauté mushrooms till the water dries.
3. Add cornflour and stir for a minute. Add milk and stir well till it forms a thick paste of spreading consistency. Remove from fire.
4. Add green chilli, salt, pepper, parsley/mint and lime juice.
5. Remove sides of the bread, roll the slices thin with rolling pin (*belan*). Spread a tablespoon of mushroom mixture on the edge of the slice and roll it up.
6. Wrap the mushrooms rolls in a damp cloth or with a cling wrap.
7. To serve, grill on greased rack in the oven for 8-10 minutes till slightly crisp. Alternately, pan fry on medium flame in a lightly greased pan, turning sides till golden.

HEALTH BENEFIT

Mushrooms are low in calories. They are rich in chromium which has positive effect on insulin.

Pita Wraps

The whole family will enjoy these for breakfast or as a snacky meal!

Makes 10 rolls

5 whole wheat pita breads

½ of a red capsicum, 1 green capsicum, ½ yellow capsicum - cut into ½" pieces

1 big onion - cut into 8 pieces and separated

4 mushrooms - cut into thick slices, ½ of a thin zucchini - cut into slightly thick slices

150 gm *paneer* - cut into fingers

MARINADE

2 tsp crushed garlic/ginger paste, 2 tsp chopped green chillies

3 tsp tomato ketchup, 2 tsp red chilli sauce, 2 tsp soya sauce, 1 tbsp olive oil, 1 tsp salt

SPREAD

1 cup yogurt - hang in a muslin cloth for 30 minutes

1 tsp garlic paste, ½ tsp each of salt, red chilli flakes and pepper

1. Mix all the ingredients of the marinade together.
2. Add all the vegetables to the marinade. Leave for 30 minutes.
3. Mix hung yogurt with all the other ingredients of the spread and keep aside.
4. Grease a large non-stick pan and keep on fire. Keeping the *paneer* aside, place all the marinated vegetables in the pan in a single layer. Pan fry without stirring too much till they get brown patches, for about 2-3 minutes. (You can do the vegetables in 2 batches also). Once the vegetables are done, add the *paneer* fingers. Mix well for a minute and remove from fire.
5. At the time of serving, slice a pita bread to make 2 rounds out of each bread. Warm the cut side on a pan for 2 minutes. Turn side and again leave it on the pan for a minute. Remove from pan.
6. On each piece of pita bread, spread 1 tbsp of prepared yogurt. Put vegetables and *paneer* on one end and roll it up. Serve.

Salads & Soups

Stir Fried Salad

Serves 4-6

1 long brinjal - cut into 1" cubes without peeling

1 zucchini - cut into 1" cubes without peeling

1 onion - cut into 1" cubes

2 cups cabbage - cut into 1" cubes

8-10 flakes garlic - sliced

3 tbsp olive oil

2 tbsp vinegar

½ tsp oregano, ½ tsp pepper, ½ tsp salt

1. Heat 1 tbsp olive oil in a non-stick pan and add the brinjals. Stir fry for 3-4 minutes till brown patches appear. Lower heat, cover and cook for 1 minute or till the brinjal pieces are cooked but firm. Remove from pan to a bowl.
2. In the same pan heat 1 tbsp oil and add zucchini. Stir fry for 2-3 minutes. Reduce heat, cover and cook till slightly tender but firm. Remove from pan to the bowl.
3. Heat 1 tbsp of oil again in the pan. Add garlic, stir and add onion, capsicum and cabbage. Stir for ½ minute till well coated in oil. Remove to the same bowl with brinjal and zucchini.
4. In a cup, mix vinegar, salt, pepper and oregano.
5. Pour over the stir fried salad and mix well. Cover with a plastic wrap. Serve cold or at room temperature.

Cucumber Cold Soup

A refreshing start to a summer meal!

Serves 2

1 cucumber

1 tbsp chopped coriander leaves

1-2 tbsp chopped mint (*pudina*)

½ cup fresh yogurt - whisked till smooth

¼ tsp black salt, ½ tsp salt

a pinch of black pepper, ¾ cup water

1. In a blender, blend cucumber, coriander, mint, salt and pepper.
2. Remove from blender. Add whisked yogurt to it.
3. Add cold water and stir. Chill. Serve cold in summers.

Spinach Orange Salad

A delightful green salad. You can substitute spinach with lettuce too or use a combination of both. Fruit adds texture and taste to the salad.

Serves 4-6

200 gms spinach (choose a firm & fresh bundle with small leaves)

2 big, firm oranges

DRESSING

2 tbsp olive oil, 1 tbsp vinegar

½ tsp light soya sauce

½ tsp salt, ½ tsp pepper, ½ tsp sugar free

TOPPING

2-3 almonds - cut into thin long pieces

1. Trim the stems of the spinach. Soak the spinach leaves for 15 minutes in a bowl of cold water to which ice cubes are added. Remove from water and pat dry on a kitchen towel. Tear into big pieces.
2. Remove the fibrous covering from each segment of orange. Keep aside.
3. Mix all the ingredients of the dressing in a small spice grinder or with a whisk till the dressing turns slightly thick.
4. Toast the almonds in a microwave for 2 minutes or on fire in a pan till fragrant. Cut almonds into slices.
5. At the time of serving, pour the dressing over the spinach, toss to mix well.
6. Lightly mix in the oranges. Remove the salad to a shallow flat bowl, top with toasted almonds. Serve immediately.

HEALTH BENEFIT

Spinach is rich in iron & calcium. Rich in folic acid, spinach is a very valuable food during pregnancy & lactation.

Chinese Vegetable Soup

A thin soup with lots of healthy veggies!

Serves 4

½ carrot - cut into thin slices diagonally

2 mushrooms - sliced

1-2 outer leaves of cabbage - cut into 1" pieces

1 tbsp oil

1 tsp grated ginger, 3 tsp crushed or finely chopped garlic

1 onion - chopped finely, 2 sticks celery - cut into ½" pieces

1 spring onion with greens - chopped (½ cup)

4 tbsp tomato puree

1 tbsp vinegar, 1 tsp soya sauce, 2 tsp red chilli sauce

1½ tsp salt, ½ tsp pepper

3 tsp cornflour

HEALTH BENEFIT

Different coloured veggies make a great health combination.

1. Heat the oil, reduce heat and add ginger and garlic. Stir for a few seconds.
2. Add onions and celery. Stir for 3-4 minutes. Add the carrot, mushrooms and cabbage. Stir for 5 minutes on high heat.
3. Add greens onion and tomato puree. Mix well for a minute.
4. Add 4 cups of boiling water. Simmer for 2 minutes.
5. Dissolve cornflour in ½ cup water and slowly add to vegetables. Also add vinegar, soya sauce, red chilli sauce, pepper and salt to taste.
6. Boil for 4-5 minutes. Serve hot.

Vegetables & Dals

Guava Subzi

It can be served as salad if cooled and kept in the refrigerator.

Serves 4

½ kg guavas (*amrood*)

1 cup yogurt - hang for ½ hour and drain the liquid

¼ tsp asafoetida (*hing*), ½ tsp cumin seeds (*jeera*)

½ tsp salt, 2 green chillies - deseeded and finely chopped

1 tsp oil, ½ tablet sugar free - powdered or ¼ tsp sugar free powder

HEALTH BENEFIT

Guava is rich in vitamin C. Helps control Blood Pressure. Rich in potassium and it is a natural way to prevent diabetes.

1. Peel guavas lightly with a peeler, cut each into 4 pieces. Remove seeds and discard them. Cut each guava into ½" pieces.
2. Heat oil in pan, add asafoetida and cumin, sauté for 2 minutes till cumin turns golden.
3. Add the guava, salt and green chillies. Remove from fire and wait for a minute to cool slightly.
4. Add yogurt and sugar free. Mix well. Serve.

Stuffed Karela

Makes 6-7

7-8 (400 gms) small sized bitter gourd (*karelas*)

3 onions - very finely chopped, 2-3 tsp oil, preferably mustard oil

DRY MASALAS

2 tsp coriander seeds (*saboot dhania*)

2 tsp fennel (*saunf*)

½ tsp fenugreek seeds (*methi daana*)

½ tsp salt, 1 tsp amchoor

½ tsp chilli powder, ½ tsp turmeric (*haldi*)

COATING

2 tsp gram flour (*besan*), 2 tsp yogurt

¼ tsp chilli powder, 1 tsp oil

1. Wash *karelas* nicely and lightly peel the karelas. Apply 1 tsp salt on the peels and keep aside. Slit karelas lengthwise and remove the seeds. If the seed are hard throw them otherwise finely chop and keep aside. Rub some salt and lemon juice inside the *karelas* and keep aside for ½ hour or even more.

2. For the filling, squeeze the salted peels nicely and wash them. Use half of the peels in the filling, the remaining half can be kneaded with flour to make a healthy dough for chappatis as given in the roti section, on page 95.

3. In a pan heat oil and saute the onion and half the *karela* peels along with seeds. Cover and cook on low flame for 10 minutes till the onions are soft. Keep stirring in-between. Remove from fire.

4. Add the dry masala to onions and let it cool.

5. Squeeze *karelas* and wash well. Squeeze again. Fill them with the masala.

6. Mix the coating ingredients.

7. Apply (smear) the coating on the stuffed karelas. Grease a large non stick pan. Arrange *karelas* in a single layer. Cover and cook on low heat for about 30 minutes, turning sides till soft and well browned all over.

Oregano Tindas

The low calorie round gourd is rich in vitamins. Oregano gives it a new flavour.

Serves 4

½ kg round gourd (*tindas*) - peel and cut each into 4 pieces

1 tsp oil, 2 onions - finely chopped, 2 tsp garlic paste

½ tsp chilli powder, 2 tsp oregano, ¾ tsp salt

2 tbsp tomato puree

1. In a pressure cooker heat oil. Add onion and sauté for 3-4 minutes and add garlic paste. Sauté for a minute.
2. Add the tindas, red chilli powder, oregano and salt. Mix well for 3-4 minutes on low heat. Add ½ cup water and pressure cook for 2 minutes on high flame. Remove from fire and let the pressure drop by itself. Open cooker.
3. Add tomato puree, mix well for 2 minutes on fire. Serve with roti.

Motiya Karela

Bitter gourds combine well with gram lentils.

Serves 4

250 gms bitter gourds (*karelas*) - lightly peel and cut into ¼" thick round slices & apply 1 tsp salt

½ cup gram lentils (*channa dal*) - soaked for 4 hours

3 onions - finely chopped

2 tsp oil, preferably mustard oil

¾ tsp salt

½ tsp red chilli powder

½ tsp turmeric (*haldi*)

1 tsp ground coriander (*dhania powder*)

1 tsp fennel (*saunf*) powder, 1 tsp dried mango powder (*amchoor*)

HEALTH BENEFIT

Bitter gourd is a wonder vegetable for diabetes. Prevents complications like hypertension, eye complications, neuritis & defective metabolism of carbohydrates.

1. Wash the salted bitter gourds 2-3 times and each time squeeze nicely.
2. Heat oil. Add the onions. Cook onions till soft and slightly brown.
3. Add bitter gourds and sauté for 5 minutes on medium flame.
4. Drain *channa dal*. Add *channa dal*, salt, red chilli and turmeric.
5. Add 3 cups water. Bring to a boil. Cover and cook for about 30 minutes till the water dries and *channa dal* is cooked. Stir in between.
6. Add ground coriander, fennel and dried mango powder. Mix well and serve.

Mint Nugget Casserole

Serves 4

1 cup nutri nugget granules (*soya keema*)

5 tomatoes (300 gms), 1 tbsp oil

2 flakes garlic - chopped, 1 bay leaf (*tej patta*)

1 whole wheat bread slice - grind in a mixer to get fresh bread crumbs (use 2 tsp crumbs and dry the rest for future use)

1 cup milk, 1 onion - chopped, ¼ cup fresh mint (*pudina*) leaves

1¼ tsp salt, ½ tsp pepper

1. Soak the nuggets in hot water for 15 minutes. Squeeze and keep aside.
2. Blanch the tomatoes in boiling water for 3-4 minutes. Remove from water and peel. Finely chop the tomatoes.
3. Heat oil in *kadhai*. Add garlic and bay leaf. Stir for a minute.

4. Add nuggets, stir fry for 4-5 minutes. Add crumbs and milk. Cook till milk boils.

5. Add onion, tomatoes and mint. Cook on slow flame for about 4-5 minutes. Add salt and pepper to taste. Serve with oat bread or whole wheat bread.

HEALTH BENEFIT

Soya - The only vegetable protein which is a complete protein. Soya lecithin contains choline, which is useful in preventing neurological complications of diabetes. Mint helps in digestion.

Cabbage with Peas

Serves 2-3

½ of a medium cabbage - cut into 1" pieces (2 cups)

¼ cup peas, 1 tomato - cut into ½" pieces

1 tsp oil

a pinch of asafoetida *(hing)*, 1 tsp fennel (*saunf)*, 2 tsp freshly grated ginger

2 tsp gram flour (*besan*)

½ tsp salt, ¼ tsp tumeric (*haldi*), 2 tsp beaten yogurt

1. In a non-stick pan heat oil, add asafoetida, fennel and ginger.
2. Add gram flour and roast for 2-3 minutes.
3. Add cabbage, peas and tomato. Cook for 2-3 minutes.
4. Add salt and turmeric. Stir for 2 minutes. Add yogurt. Cook for 7-8 minutes on slow fire till done. Serve.

Jhatpat Kaddu

The green variety of pumpkin is a better choice as it is less sweet.

Serves 3-4

½ kg green pumpkin (*kaddu*) - cut into small cubes, see note

1 onion - finely chopped

1½ tsp panchphoran spices or achaari spices (or mix together - ½ tsp cumin (*jeera*)

½ tsp mustard (*rai*), ¼ tsp onion seeds (*kalonji*)

¼ tsp fennel (*saunf*) and a pinch of fenugreek seeds (*methi dana*)

½ tsp *amchoor*, 1 tsp salt

½ tsp turmeric (*haldi*)

1 tsp oil, ½ cup water

1. Heat oil in a non-stick pan. Add the panchphoran spices. Cook till fennel (*saunf*) changes colour and turns light golden.
2. Add chopped onion and sauté for 2 minutes. Add salt and turmeric.
3. Add pumpkin and sauté for 6-8 minutes on low flame. Add water, cook covered for 15 minutes on slow fire till it is cooked.
4. Add *amchoor* and mix well.

Note: The peel of pumpkin adds to the crunch as well as nutrition. It is a good idea to peel half the vegetable and keep the other half with the peel.

HEALTH BENEFIT

Pumpkin is rich in vitamin A. Latest Chinese research found consumption of pumpkin reduces the intake of insulin.

Lauki aur Matar Milan

An unusual combination of bottle gourd and green peas.

Serves 4

½ of a small, thin bottle gourd (*lauki*), total weight of *lauki* 250 gm - cut piece into half lengthwise & then cut into ¾" thick slices (1 cup)

½ cup boiled peas, 1 tsp oil

1 tsp cumin seeds (*jeera*), 1 tbsp garlic paste, ½ tsp ginger paste

MASALA

1 tbsp oil, 1 onion - chopped finely

¾ tsp salt, 1 tsp ground coriander *(dhania powder)*

¼ tsp turmeric (*haldi*), ¼ tsp red chilli powder

1 tsp garlic paste, 1 tomato - chopped finely, 3-4 tbsp tomato puree

GRIND TOGETHER

1 tsp fennel (*saunf*), 2 green cardamoms (*chhoti illaichi*), ½ tsp cumin seeds (*jeera*)

1. Boil gourd in 8 cups water with 1½ tsp salt for 10 minutes till soft. Strain. Refresh in cold water.
2. Heat 1 tsp oil. Add 1 tsp cumin. When it turns golden, add 1 tbsp garlic paste and ½ tsp ginger paste. Stir for a minute. Add boiled gourd. Saute for 2-3 minutes.
3. For the masala, cook onions with 1 tbsp in a nonstick pan on low heat till light brown. Add chopped tomatoes. Stir well. Add 3-4 tbsp tomato puree.
4. Add salt, 1 tsp coriander powder, ¼ tsp turmeric, ¼ tsp red chilli powder and 1 tsp garlic paste. Cook on low heat for 5-7 minutes.
5. Add the gourd and boiled peas to the masala. Mix well.
6. Add ground fennel, cardamom and cumin. Toss lightly and serve.

Methi Amrood ki Subzi

Fenugreek and guavas - a unique combination!

Serves 3-4

1 bunch (500 gms) fenugreek greens (*methi*) - chop leaves finely

2 guavas (*amroods*) - cut into 4 pieces, remove seeds and then cut into ¼" pieces

½ tsp cumin seeds (*jeera*), 2 dry, red chillies - broken

1 tsp finely chopped ginger

1 large onion - chopped finely

1 tsp coriander (*dhania*) powder

¼ tsp turmeric (*haldi*), ½ tsp salt to taste, ½ tsp *garam masala*

1 tomato - chopped finely

1 tbsp oil

1. Boil 4 cups water with 2 tsp salt in a *kadhai*. Add fenugreek leaves and boil for 5-6 minutes on low heat till soft. Drain, refresh in cold water and keep aside.
2. Heat oil in a non stick pan or *kadhai*. Add cumin, broken red chillies and chopped ginger. Stir and add the onions. Cook till light brown. Add coriander powder, turmeric, salt and *garam masala*. Stir for a minute.
3. Add the tomato and cook for 3-4 minutes on low heat. Add guavas. Stir for 2 minutes. Add ½ cup water, cover and simmer the masala on low heat for about 5-7 minutes, till well blended and guavas are cooked.
4. Add boiled fenugreek leaves and ¼ tsp salt. Stir fry fenugreek leaves for 5-6 minutes. Serve hot.

HEALTH BENEFIT

Fenugreek leaves help in the insulin utilization and stabilizes the glucose level. Good for digestion too.

Achaari Broccoli & Pumpkin

Serves 4

250 gms pumpkin (*kaddu*) - cut into 1" pieces

150 gms (1 medium) broccoli - cut into florets

2 onions - chopped roughly

1 firm tomato - cut into 8 pieces and remove pulp

ACHAARI TEMPERING

1-2 red chillies - broken in ½" pieces

¾ tsp onion seeds (*kalonji*), ½ tsp fenugreek seeds (*methi dana*)

¾ tsp cumin seeds (*jeera*), ¾ tsp mustard seeds (*rai*), ¾ tsp fennel (*saunf*)

OTHER INGREDIENTS

2 tbsp oil, ½ tsp *amchoor* powder, ½ tsp sugar free powder, ¼ tsp salt, or to taste

½ tsp chilli powder, ¼ tsp turmeric (*haldi*), 1 tsp ground coriander (*dhania powder)*

HEALTH BENEFIT

A healthy combination of green & yellow vegetables. Broccoli is a rich source of calcium & a great anti-oxidant.

1. Boil 1½ cups water with ½ tsp salt. Add broccoli and cook for 2 minutes till crisp tender. Remove from water and keep aside.
2. Collect all the *achaari masalas*.
3. Heat oil in a *kadhai* and add the *achaari masalas.* After a minute, add the onions and cook till light brown.
4. Add salt, turmeric, ground coriander and chilli powder. Stir for a few seconds. Add pumpkin and stir fry for a minute. Add ¼ cup water. Cover and cook for about 10 minutes till pumpkin is tender but holds its shape.
5. Sprinkle sugar free and *amchoor.* Mix well. Add the broccoli and tomatoes. Cook for 2-3 minutes and serve hot.

Baked Spinach Paneer

Paneer topped with roasted tomatoes on a bed of spinach.

Serves 4-5

200 gms *paneer* - cut into ¼" cubes, 1 tsp oregano

½ kg spinach - shred leaves finely

1 onion - chopped finely, 3-4 big flakes garlic - chopped finely (3 tsp)

1-2 green chillies - chopped finely

1 tsp oil

2 cups milk, 3 tsp cornflour

½ tsp cinnamon (*dalchini*) powder, ½ tsp black pepper, 1 tsp salt

TOMATO TOPPING

3 tomatoes - roasted on fire, peeled and chopped, 1 onion - finely chopped

2 tbsp tomato puree, ½ tsp salt

1 tbsp chopped fresh coriander, ½ tablet sugar free - crushed

1. In a pan stir fry onions and garlic. Cook till soft. Wash and add spinach. Add green chillies and cook for 10-12 minutes till soft.
2. Dissolve cornflour, cinnamon, black pepper and salt in milk and add to the cooked spinach. Bring to a boil and cook for about 10 minutes till slightly thick.
3. In a greased baking dish pour the spinach mixture. Spread the *paneer* pieces over it. Sprinkle oregano. Keep aside.
4. To prepare the tomato topping, roast tomatoes on a naked flame till slightly blackened. Let them cool. Remove the skin of tomatoes and finely chop them. In a pan cook all ingredients of the topping except the coriander and sweetener till thick, for about 15 minutes till it attains a thick paste like consistency. Remove from fire and add coriander and sweetener.
5. Spread the tomato topping on the *paneer* in the dish. Bake covered with foil at 180°C/350°F for 10-12 minutes. Serve hot with a bread.

Baked Broccoli

Serves 2

1 medium broccoli - cut into florets (2 cups), reserve the stalk, 1 tbsp lemon juice, 2 onions - chopped
2 tbsp gram flour (*besan*) - roasted for a minute on low heat, 1½ cups milk
2 tbsp fresh basil, 1 tsp salt, ½ tsp black pepper, 2 tbsp bread crumbs, 2 tbsp grated cheese

1. Peel the stalk of the broccoli and cut into thin round slices. Boil 4 cups water with 1 tsp salt and 1 tbsp lemon juice. Add broccoli florets and stalks to hot water and boil for 5 minutes till soft. Remove from water and rinse in cold water.
2. Dissolve the gram flour with milk and keep aside.
3. Heat 1 tsp oil in a non-stick pan and stir fry the broccoli and stalks for 3-4 minutes. Add milk slowly and let it boil for 2-3 minutes. Add bread crumbs and mix well. Add basil, salt and pepper. Transfer to a greased baking dish. Finely grate some cheese on it.
4. Bake in a preheated oven at 180°C/350°F for 4-5 minutes. Grill for 2 minutes. Serve.

Ajwaini Phalli

Beans tossed with carom seeds.

Serves 4

½ kg green beans (*guar phalli*) - cut into 1" pieces

2 tsp oil, preferably mustard oil

a pinch of asafoetida (*hing*)

½ tsp turmeric (*haldi*)

½ tsp fenugreek seeds (*methi dana*)

½ tsp cumin seeds (*jeera*)

¾ tsp carom seeds (*ajwain*)

5-6 flakes garlic - crushed

¾ tsp red chilli

¾ tsp *amchoor*

juice of half lemon (2 tsp juice)

1. Boil 4 cups water with 1 tsp salt. Add *guar phalli* and boil for about 10 minutes till soft. Remove from water and refresh with cold water to preserve the colour.

2. Heat oil. Add asafoetida, turmeric, fenugreek seeds, cumin seeds and carom seeds. Cook till cumin is golden brown.

3. Add crushed garlic. Mix well. Add *guar phalli* and ½ tsp salt. Mix well. Add ¼ cup water and cook for 5-7 minutes. Add red chilli powder and *amchoor*.

4. To serve, heat vegetable and add lemon juice.

Mix Vegetable Saag

Serves 4

250 gms fenugreek greens (*methi*) - chopped

1 bunch, about 500 gm spinach (*paalak*) - shred leaves roughly

1 large carrot - peeled and chopped

1 cup chopped bottle gourd (*lauki*)

1 medium cucumber (*kheera*) - chopped

3 tsp oil, 5-6 flakes garlic - chopped

3 green chillies - chopped

1" piece ginger - chopped, 1 onion - chopped

2 tomatoes - chopped

1 tsp red chilli powder, 2 tsp coriander (*dhania*) powder

½ tsp turmeric (*haldi*), ½ tsp *garam masala*, 1 tsp salt

1. Wash spinach and fenugreek greens together.

2. Heat 3 tsp oil in a deep pan or a *kadhai*. Add garlic and saute for 2 minutes. Add ginger, green chillies and onion. Saute for 2-3 minutes.

3. Add tomatoes. Stir for 2 minutes. Add all the dry masalas and salt.

4. Add carrot, gourd, cucumber, fenugreek and spinach. Mix well. Add 1 cup water. Bring to a boil. Cover and cook on medium heat for about 10 minutes, until the vegetables turn soft and almost dry. Remove from fire and let it cool.

5. Transfer all the vegetables in a blender. Grind to a coarse paste, using a little warm water. Serve saag hot with roti.

HEALTH BENEFIT

Enjoy the benefits of mixed greens. Cucumber is a natural diuretics, promoting the flow of urine.

Achaari Amla Subzi

Gooseberry with Indian pickle spices. Stays for 10-12 days in the refrigerator.

Serves 4

250 gms Indian goose berry (*amla*)

1 tsp oil, preferably mustard oil

½ tsp fenugreek seeds (*methi dana*)

2 tsp fennel (*saunf*), ½ tsp cumin (*jeera*)

1 tsp salt, ¼ tsp turmeric (*haldi*), ¾ tsp red chilli

1 tsp dry fenugreek (*kasoori methi*)

1. Wash *amlas* and microwave covered for 5 minutes. Make a cut and press to remove the seeds. Cut into thin slices.

2. Heat oil, add fenugreek seeds, fennel and cumin. When cumin turns light brown, add *amla*, salt, turmeric, red chilli powder and dry fenugreek leaves. Mix well and cook for 2 minutes.

Sweet and Sour Karelas

Tamarind, rich in vitamin C, acts as an antioxidant. It reduces the bitterness of karelas too and makes them more delicious.

Serves 4

200 gms bitter gourds (*karelas*), 1" ball of tamarind - soak in hot water and remove pulp (3 tbsp)

2 tsp oil, ½ tsp carom seeds (*ajwain*), 3 onions - sliced thinly

½ tsp salt, ½ tsp red chilli, 1 tablet sugar free - crushed

1. Cut the bitter gourds into thin slices. Apply 1 tsp salt and leave for 1 hour. Wash them. Squeeze the water nicely from the bitter gourds.
2. Heat oil in non-stick pan. Add carom seeds and saute for ½ minute. Add onions and sauté for a few minutes till light brown.
3. Add bitter gourds and ½ tsp salt. Mix well. Cover and cook for 15-20 minutes till cooked. Keep stirring in between. Add red chilli powder, 3 tbsp tamarind pulp, ¼ cup water. Remove from fire. Add sugar free. Mix well and serve hot.

Grilled Masala Gobhi

Tamarind and coconut masala make this dish of cauliflower special.

Serves 4

1 small cauliflower (*gobhi*) - cut into medium florets

½ of a coconut - grated (1 cup)

a tiny ball of tamarind - soak in ¼ cup water and extract

2 tbsp pulp

2 tbsp tomato ketchup

2 tbsp oil, 3 onions - chopped very finely

½ cup curry leaves

1" piece ginger - chopped (1½ tbsp)

4-6 flakes garlic - chopped (1 tbsp)

1 tsp red chilli powder, 1 tsp salt

1. Grate half of the coconut. Divide the grated coconut into two portions. To one part, add 1 cup hot water. Grind in a mixer and strain through a muslin cloth to extract coconut milk.
2. To the remaining half of the grated coconut, add tamarind, garlic, salt, red chilli and curry leaves. Grind to a paste and keep aside.
3. Boil 4 cups water with 1 tsp salt and add cauliflower florets to it. Boil for about 10 minutes till fully cooked. Remove from fire and strain. Pat dry the cauliflower.
4. Marinate cauliflower in the coconut-tamarind masala.
5. Heat 2 tbsp oil. Sauté the onions till light golden brown. Add coconut milk and tomato ketchup. Keep aside.
6. Grease a baking dish. Arrange cauliflower in the masala in the dish. Pour the coconut milk and onion mixture. Grill for 5-7 minutes till golden. Serve hot.

HEALTH BENEFIT

Consumption of curry leaves is good for diabetes and high blood pressure. These leaves add nutrition & great taste to the low calorie cauliflower.

Tulsi Tori Paneer

Basil adds the herb touch to the gourd vegetable. Paneer gives the dish proteins.

Serves 4

250 gms *tori or* zucchini - peeled lightly and cut into ¼" thick round slices

150 gms *paneer* - cut into ¼" cubes, 10-15 *tulsi* leaves

1 tbsp oil, 1" piece ginger - chopped finely, 1 onion - finely sliced, ¼ tsp turmeric (*haldi*)

1 tomato - chopped, 1 green chilli - finely chopped, 1 tsp salt, ½ tsp ground pepper, 1 tsp lemon juice

1. Heat oil in pressure cooker, add ginger and fry for a minute, add the onions and stir fry for another minute.
2. Add turmeric. Stir for a minute. Add tomato and stir for 2-3 minutes.
3. Add *tori* and green chillies. Cook for 2-3 minutes.
4. Add salt and *tulsi*. Mix well. Add ¼ cup water and pressure cook for 5 minutes.
5. Remove from fire and let the pressure drop. Add *paneer*, pepper and lemon juice. Serve hot.

Stuffed Tinda

The round gourd with a special flavour and texture.

Serves 4

½ kg round gourd (*tindas*)

1 tsp oil, a pinch of asafoetida (*hing*)

MIX TOGETHER

1½ cups curd, 2 tsp gram flour (*besan)*

2 tsp crushed garlic, ½ tsp salt

3 tsp dry fenugreek leaves (*kasoori methi*)

MASALA

1 tsp coriander seeds (*saboot dhania*)

1 tsp fennel (*saunf*), 2-3 dry red chillies

½ tsp salt, ½ tsp turmeric (*haldi*)

1. Peel the *tindas*. Make 2 cross cuts, leaving the base intact. Do not cut till the end.
2. Dry roast coriander seeds, fennel and dry red chillies to a coarse powder. Add ½ tsp each of salt and turmeric.
3. Fill the dry masala in *tindas*.
4. Crush the garlic, add to beaten curds. Also add salt, dry fenugreek leaves and gram flour.
5. Marinate the *tindas* in the curd for 15-20 minutes.
6. In a pressure cooker heat oil, add a pinch of asafoetida. Reduce heat. Add the marinated tindas along with the curd. Bhuno constantly on low heat for 5 minutes. Pressure cook to give one whistle. As soon as the whistle comes or the pressure develops, remove from fire and let the pressure drop by itself. Serve hot.

Moong Dal with Carrot & Beans

Enjoy the colour and taste of these vegetables in your everyday cooking.

Serves 4

1 cup skinned split *moong* beans (*dhuli moong dal*)

½ cup carrots cut into ¼" cubes, ½ cup beans cut into ¼" cubes

2 green chillies - finely chopped

1 tbsp oil, 1 onion - finely chopped, 2 tsp crushed garlic

1½ tsp salt, ½ tsp turmeric (*haldi*), 1 tsp ground cumin (*jeera powder*), 1 tsp coriander (*dhania*) powder

ADD LATER

½ tsp garam masala, 1 tbsp chopped coriander

1 tomato - cut into 4 pieces, remove seeds and chop

1. Wash the *dal* and soak in 4 cups water for 15 minutes.
2. In a pressure cooker, heat oil. Add garlic and onion. Sauté for 3-4 minutes.

3. Add carrots and beans. Cook for 2-3 minutes. Add green chillies. Stir.

4. Add dal with water to it. Add salt, turmeric, cumin and coriander powder.

5. Close the cooker and pressure cook for 2-3 minutes after the pressure forms.

6. After the pressure drops, add garam masala, tomato and coriander. Serve.

HEALTH BENEFIT

Moong dal is easy to digest. Carrots & beans enrich the dal with vitamin A. Beans are good for diabetes.

Lauki in Tomato Gravy

Bottle gourd in a quick tomato curry. Any vegetable can be added to the gravy.

Serves 4

500 gm bottle gourd (*lauki*)

1 tbsp oil

1 tsp tomato ketchup, optional

½ tsp degi mirch, ½ tsp ground cumin (*jeera powder*), ½ tsp salt

GRAVY

2 onions - roughly chopped, 4 tomatoes - roughly chopped

3-4 garlic flakes - chopped, 1" piece ginger - chopped

1" piece cinnamon (*dalchini*), 3 cloves (*laung*)

4–5 black pepper corns (*saboot kali mirch*)

10 almonds soaked in water for 1 hour - peeled and chopped roughly

1. Peel and cut bottle gourd into round slices. Cut each slice into 2 pieces. Remove the centre seedy portion. Boil 2 cups water with ½ tsp salt. Add bottle gourd and boil for 5-7 minutes till soft. Keep the liquid aside. Refresh bottle gourd in cold water. Keep aside.

2. For the gravy, boil together all ingredients except almonds with ½ cup water for 3-4 minutes or pressure cook for 1 whistle. After they cool down, add the almonds and grind together to a paste.

3. Heat oil in a *kadhai*, cook paste for 3-4 minutes, till dry. Add 1 tbsp oil and stir the masala for 2-3 minutes. Add 1½ cups of the reserved water to make the gravy. Boil.

4. Add *degi mirch*, cumin powder and salt to taste. Simmer for 2-3 minutes. Add the bottle gourd. Mix well. Add ketchup if you like. Serve hot with chappatis.

Dal Medley

Vegetables added to mixed lentils add more nutrition to the already healthy food.

Serves 4

PRESSURE COOK TOGETHER

¼ cup gram lentils (*chana dal*), ¼ cup yellow lentils (*arhar dal*)

2 tbsp red lentils (*masoor dal*)

½ onion - chopped

3" (100 gms) pumpkin - chopped (½ cup), 100 gms bottle gourd (*lauki*) - chopped (½ cup)

2 garlic flakes - chopped, ½" piece ginger - grated or finely chopped

¾ tsp salt, 1 tsp chilli powder, 2 cups water

TEMPERING (*TADKA*)

1 tsp oil, ½ tsp cumin seeds (*jeera*), a pinch of asafoetida (*hing*)

1 tsp dry fenugreek leaves (*kasoori methi*), 2 tsp sambar powder

1 tsp lemon juice

1. Wash all the dals. Place all the ingredients and water in a pressure cooker. Keep on fire. After the pressure forms, cook for 4-5 minutes. Remove from fire and let the pressure drop by itself.

2. For tempering, heat oil. Add the asafoetida and cumin. Fry till cumin turns brown. Add dry fenugreek leaves and sambar powder. Mix. Pour *tadka* over *dal*. Add lemon juice and mix well.

HEALTH BENEFIT

Vegetables added to the dal makes it more nutritious. Foods good for diabetes like pumpkin, garlic & fenugreek have been used in the recipe.

Rotis & Rice

Karela Roti

Enjoy the health benefit of the peels of bitter gourd without the bitter taste.

Makes 6

1 cup whole wheat flour (*atta*), ½ cup soya flour

½ cup gram flour (*besan*), ½ cup karela peels

1 onion - finely chopped, 1 tsp salt

1. Mix the above ingredients and make a chappati dough with water. Knead well and keep covered for 30 minutes. Make chappatis with the prepared dough.

Kasoori Roti

Fenugreek - dry or fresh, adds a special taste to the dough.

HEALTH BENEFIT

Soya bean flour, gram flour (*besan*) and bajra can be incorporated into the wheat flour for making chappatis. This enhances the protein value and fibre content

Makes 6

1 cup whole wheat flour (*atta*), ½ cup soya flour

2 tbsp yogurt

3 tbsp dry fenugreek leaves (*kasoori methi*) or 1 cup fresh fenugreek greens (*methi*)

½ tsp chilli powder, a pinch turmeric (*haldi*), ½ tsp salt

1. Soak the dry fenugreek leaves in ¼ cup water for 15-20 minutes.
2. Mix the flours with all ingredients — spices, yogurt and the soaked or fresh fenugreek. Knead to a smooth dough. Keep aside for an hour.
3. Divide dough into 6 portions. Roll out chappatis and cook on a hot *tawa*.

Oat Bran Mooli Roti

Oat bran which is rich in soluble fibre is mixed with an equal volume of flour. Filling is important, as the roti becomes a little hard to enjoy if made without any filling.

Makes 6

1 cup whole wheat flour (*atta*), 1 cup oat bran

1 radish (*mooli*) along with the green leaves - grate radish and finely chop the leaves

salt and red chilli powder to taste

1. Make a dough using equal quantities of flour and oat bran. Keep aside covered for 30 minutes. (You can mix larger quantities of both and store in a container.)
2. Squeeze grated radish and mix the green leaves. Add salt and red chilli powder to taste. Make a stuffed roti using radish as the filling. Serve.

Missi Mooli ki Roti

Makes 6

1 cup whole wheat flour (*atta*), 1 cup gram flour (*besan*)

a pinch of carom seeds (*ajwain*), a pinch of turmeric (*haldi*), ¼ tsp salt

radish (*mooli*) filling as given on page 97

1. Make a dough with wheat flour, gram flour, carom seeds, turmeric and salt. Keep aside covered for 30 minutes.
2. Make filling as given on page 97. Make a stuffed roti with the above dough using radish as the filling. Serve.

Spiced Paalak Roti

Makes 8

1 cup whole wheat flour (*atta*), ½ cup gram flour (*besan*), ½ cup *bajra* (optional)

1 tsp fenugreek seeds (*methi dana*) & 1 tsp fennel (*saunf*) - grind together to a powder

1 cup finely chopped spinach (*paalak*), 1 onion - finely chopped

1½ tsp chopped ginger, 1½ tsp chopped garlic

1 tsp onion seeds (*kalonji*)

1 tsp salt, 1 tsp red chilli, 1 tsp *amchoor*, 1 tsp ground coriander (*dhania*)

1. Mix all the above ingredients and form a dough of rolling consistency. Keep aside covered for 30 minutes. Make chappatis and serve hot.

Nugget Pulao

Diabetics benefit from carbohydrates which are rich in fibre and brown rice falls in the good carbohydrate category.

Serves 4

1 cup brown rice

½ cup nutrela granules (*soya bean*) - soak for 15-20 minutes

½ cup chopped french beans, 1 carrot - cut into small cubes

½ cup small florets of cauliflower

¼ cup tomato puree, 1 onion - chopped fine

1 tbsp oil, ½ tsp whole peppercorns (*saboot kali mirch*)

1" stick cinnamon (*dalchini*), 1 bay leaf (*tej patta*), 2-3 cloves (*laung*)

1 tsp ginger paste, 1 tsp garlic paste

2 tsp salt or to taste

¾ tsp *garam masala* powder

1. Wash rice and keep aside.
2. Soak soya granules in hot water for 15-20 minutes. Strain and squeeze well through a strainer.
3. Heat 1 tbsp oil in a heavy bottom pan. Add whole peppercorns, stir for a minute. Add onions, cinnamon, bay leaf and cloves. Fry till onions turn brown.
4. Add ginger and garlic paste. Fry for 1 minute.
5. Add drained soya granules to browned onions. Add tomato puree, salt and garam masala. Fry for 3-4 minutes till dry
6. Add vegetables and stir fry for 2-3 minutes.
7. Add rice and 3 cups water. Bring to a good boil.
8. Cover the pan of rice with a well fitting lid. Cook on low heat for about 22-25 minutes till the rice is done and the water gets absorbed. Remove from heat and keep covered for 5 minutes. Serve.

Raitas, Pickles & Chutneys

Jamun Chutney

Serves 4-6

500 gm jambul fruit (*jamun*), ½ cup water

2 tsp oil, 2 tsp grated ginger

½ tsp pepper, 1 tsp salt, ¼ tsp black salt (*kala namak*), 1 tsp citric acid

4 tablets sugar free, or to taste - crushed

1. Boil *jamun* in ½ cup water for 5-7 minutes till tender. Remove from fire. Add citric acid. Mix and let it cool.
2. Mash *jamuns*, removing the seed.
3. Heat 2 tsp oil. Add ginger and saute for a minute. Add *jamun* pulp and cook till you get a chutney consistency.
4. Add salt, pepper and sugar free to taste. It can be refrigerated for a few days.

Guava Raita

A good way to consume the healthy fruit.

Serves 4

2 cups yogurt

1 ripe guava

¼ tsp black salt (*kala namak*), ¼ tsp salt

1 tsp roasted cumin (*bhuna jeera*) powder

1 tbsp chopped coriander, ¼-½ tsp sugar free

1. Peel the guava. Grate guava from all sides till you reach the centre seedy portion. Discard the seeds part.
2. Beat the yogurt and add salt and spices. Add sugar free to taste.
3. Add the grated guava and garnish with coriander and cumin.

Amla Pickle

Makes 1 small jar

200 gm Indian goose berry (*amla*)

¼ cup mustard oil, 2 tsp fennel (*saunf*), 1½ tsp brown mustard (*rai*)

½ tsp fenugreek seeds (*methi dana*), ½ tsp onion seeds (*kalonji*), 1 tsp salt

1 tsp red chilli powder, ¼-½ tsp turmeric (*haldi*)

1. Wash amlas well. Prick deeply with a fork. Soak amlas in 3 cups water and 2 tsp salt for about 1 hour.
2. Heat oil to smoking point. Remove from fire. Add whole spices — fennel, mustard seeds, fenugreek seeds and onion seeds. Wait for a minute.
3. Add turmeric and mix well. Add amlas. Stir fry for 5 minutes on medium heat.
4. Add salt and red chilli powder. Mix well and remove from fire.
5. Transfer to a jar. Keep in the sun for 5-6 days.

Sweet Dishes

It is suggested that sweet dishes made with sugar free are consumed within 24 hours.

Stewed Guava Cups

Cinnamon adds natural sweetness to this fruity dessert.

Serves 8

4 small, ripe but firm, guavas (*amrood*)

2 cups water, 1" stick cinnamon (*dalchini*)

1 tsp lemon juice

½ tsp sugar free powder

FILLING

1½ cups milk

1 tsp cornflour, a pinch of saffron (*kesar*) - soaked in 1 tsp hot water

3-4 tbsp finely grated *paneer*, a pinch of ground cinnamon (*dalchini*) powder

sugar free to taste

GARNISH

1-2 chopped pistas and almonds

1. Wash the guavas well. Peel them. Cut the guavas into half and scoop out the seeds to get 8 cups or shells. Discard seeds.

2. Put 2 cups water, cinnamon stick, 1 tsp lemon juice and sugar free powder in a pan. Bring to a boil. Add the guava cups and bring to a boil again. Lower heat and cover. Keep them covered on fire for 1-2 minutes only, till they are crisp-tender. They should be soft but still hold their shape. Let guavas be in water for 5 minutes. Remove the guava shells from the water. Drain syrup well and arrange guavas in a serving dish.

3. For the filling, mix milk with cornflour and saffron. Cook milk in a thick bottomed pan or a *kadhai*. After the boil, keep on low heat and simmer till slightly thick and creamy. Do not make it too thick. Remove from heat and cool for 1-2 minutes. Add the finely grated *paneer* and cinnamon. Add sugar free to taste. Mix well. Add enough *paneer* to get a rabri consistency.

4. To assemble, pour the filling in the guava cups arranged in the serving platter. Garnish with chopped pistachio and almonds. Refrigerate. Serve chilled.

Lauki & Carrot Kheer

Rice has been substituted with veggies like bottle gourd and carrots in this dessert.

Serves 2-3

2½ cups skim milk

½ cup finely grated carrot

½ cup finely grated bottle gourd (*lauki*) - peel thickly and then finely grate

3 tsp sugar free

1 tsp cornflour dissolved in ¼ cup water

¼ tsp green cardamom (*chhoti illaichi*) powder

1 tsp raisins (*kishmish*), optional

3-4 almonds - sliced thinly

TO GARNISH

½ apple - cut into thin slices with the peel

1. To make *chenna*, heat milk till it boils. Add lemon juice. Stir till milk completely curdles. Hang *chenna* in a muslin cloth for ½ hour to drain out all the water.
2. Mix sugar free, saffron and cardamom powder to the *chenna* and rub well with the palms, till it becomes very smooth.
3. Add the finely sliced almonds and grated pineapple to it and make into flattened balls.
4. Decorate with thinly sliced almonds and sprinkle a pinch of cardamom powder.

Chenna Kulfi

The khoa is substituted with low fat paneer.

Serves 12

1 kg (5 cups) skimmed milk - at room temperature

4 tbsp sugar free, or to taste

2 tbsp cornflour

75 gm *paneer* - grated finely (¾ cup)

seeds of 3-4 green cardamoms (*chhoti illaichi*) - crushed

1 tbsp raisins (*kishmish*) - chopped finely, optional

1 tbsp shredded almonds (*badam*)

TO DECORATE

a few threads of saffron (*kesar*)

a few chopped pista

1. Dissolve cornflour in ¼ cup milk.
2. Boil the rest of the milk. Keep on fire for about 20-25 minutes, till reduced to half the quantity.
3. Add crushed cardamoms.
4. Add the cornflour paste to the boiling milk, stirring continuously.
5. Continue boiling, by lowering the flame, for about 2-3 minutes. Remove from fire. Add sugar free. Mix very well. Cool the mixture.
6. Add *paneer*, raisins and almonds. Check sweetness.
7. Fill in clean kulfi moulds and leave to set in the freezer for 6-8 hours.
8. Serve topped with saffron and pista.

Mocha Chocolate Mousse

A great combination of coffee and chocolate!

Serves 4-5

2½ cups skim milk, 5 tbsp cocoa powder, 1 tbsp cornflour

1½ cups thick curd - hang for ½ hour in a muslin cloth and squeeze lightly

2 tsp coffee dissolved in 3 tbsp hot water

5 tsp sugar free powder

3 tsp gelatine

1 tsp vanilla essence

1. Dissolve cocoa and cornflour in ¼ cup warm water to make a thick paste. Add cocoa paste to milk. Mix well. Keep on fire. Cook, stirring continuously till the milk turns slightly thick, like custard and coats the spoon. Remove from fire.
2. Add coffee paste. Mix well. Keep chocolate custard aside.

3. Sprinkle gelatine on ¼ cup water kept in a small pan. Stir on low flame till gelatine dissolves. Remove from fire and add hot gelatine to the hot chocolate custard. Mix well. Keep aside to come to room temperature.

4. Whip hung curd, essence and sugar free with an electric beater till smooth. Add the curd mix to the cooled chocolate custard and mix well.

5. Check sweetness. Add 1-2 tsp sugar free if required, depending on the sourness of the curd. Transfer to individual serving glasses or a bowl and keep in the fridge for 3-4 hours or till set. Garnish with a cherry.

Almond Panna Cotta

This delicate Italian dessert glows like a jewel with almonds and strawberries. Cream is replaced by fresh cream-cheese (chhena) prepared by curdling skim milk.

Serves 10

1 litre skim milk, 2 tbsp vinegar

2 cups curd (yogurt) - hang in a muslin cloth for 20-30 minutes

4 tsp gelatine

8-10 almonds - blanched (soaked in hot water and peeled) and very finely chopped

1 cup milk, 8 tsp sugar free, 2 drops sweet almond essence

RUBY SAUCE (OPTIONAL)

1 cup freshly pureed strawberries, 1 tsp cornflour, 1 tsp sugar free, or to taste

1. Boil milk. Reduce heat. Add vinegar so as to curdle milk. Remove from heat and strain to get home made *paneer*.

2. Place hung curd, *paneer* and milk in a blender and blend to a smooth paste. Remove to a bowl.

3. Sprinkle gelatine on ½ cup water. Heat gently (do not bring to boil) till gelatine dissolves. Remove from fire. Add sugar free to gelatine. Mix well to dissolve.

4. Add the hot gelatine solution gradually, stirring continuously with the other hand, to the yogurt mixture. Mix well. Let it cool to room temperature.

5. Add essence and blanched almonds. Check sweetness.

6. Transfer to a serving dish. If you want to unmould the dessert for individual serving, rinse small glass bowls or tart moulds with water and do not wipe. Transfer the above mixture to the wet bowls or tart mould. Keep in the fridge to set well, for about 3-4 hours.

7. After it is set, prepare the sauce. Mix strawberry puree and cornflour and cook till sauce coats the back of a spoon and attains a thick pouring consistency. Remove from fire. Add sugar free to taste. Cool.

8. Decorate the set dessert by pouring sauce with a spoon to make diagonal lines or diamonds on the set dessert. Arrange strawberry halves. Sprinkle toasted almonds. Serve chilled.

Glossary of Names/Terms

Appetizers	Small tasty bits of food served before meals.
Aubergine	Brinjal/eggplant
Au gratin	Any dish made with white sauce and covered with cheese and then baked or grilled.
Baste	To brush the food with some fat during cooking in the oven, to keep it moist and soft.
Batter	Any mixture of flour and a liquid which is beaten or stirred to make a pouring consistency.
Bell peppers	Capsicums
Blanch	To remove skin by dipping into hot water for a couple of minutes. e.g. to blanch tomatoes or almonds.
Curry powder	A blend of Indian spices.
Desiccated coconut	Powdered coconut.
Dice	To cut into small neat cubes.
Dough	A mixture of flour, liquid etc., kneaded together into a stiff paste or roll.
Drain	To remove liquid from food.
Marinate	To soak food in a mixture for some time so that flavours penetrates into the food.
Minced	Very finely chopped.
Okra	A green vegetable, also called lady finger.
Plain flour	All purpose flour, *maida*.
Saute	To toss and make light brown in shallow fat.
Soup cubes	Flavourful cubes added to soups or sauces. Also called seasoning cubes or stock cubes.
Tofu	Cheese prepared by curdling soya bean milk.

INTERNATIONAL CONVERSION GUIDE

These are not exact equivalents; they've been rounded-off to make measuring easier.

WEIGHTS & MEASURES

METRIC	*IMPERIAL*
15 g	½ oz
30 g	1 oz
60 g	2 oz
90 g	3 oz
125 g	4 oz (¼ lb)
155 g	5 oz
185 g	6 oz
220 g	7 oz
250 g	8 oz (½ lb)
280 g	9 oz
315 g	10 oz
345 g	11 oz
375 g	12 oz (¾ lb)
410 g	13 oz
440 g	14 oz
470 g	15 oz
500 g	16 oz (1 lb)
750 g	24 oz (1½ lb)
1 kg	30 oz (2 lb)

LIQUID MEASURES

METRIC	*IMPERIAL*
30 ml	1 fluid oz
60 ml	2 fluid oz
100 ml	3 fluid oz
125 ml	4 fluid oz
150 ml	5 fluid oz (¼ pint/1 gill)
190 ml	6 fluid oz
250 ml	8 fluid oz
300 ml	10 fluid oz (½ pint)
500 ml	16 fluid oz
600 ml	20 fluid oz (1 pint)
1000 ml	1¾ pints

CUPS & SPOON MEASURES

METRIC	*IMPERIAL*
1 ml	¼ tsp
2 ml	½ tsp
5 ml	1 tsp
15 ml	1 tbsp
60 ml	¼ cup
125 ml	½ cup
250 ml	1 cup

HELPFUL MEASURES

METRIC	*IMPERIAL*
3 mm	1/8 in
6 mm	¼ in
1 cm	½ in
2 cm	¾ in
2.5 cm	1 in
5 cm	2 in
6 cm	2½ in
8 cm	3 in
10 cm	4 in
13 cm	5 in
15 cm	6 in
18 cm	7 in
20 cm	8 in
23 cm	9 in
25 cm	10 in
28 cm	11 in
30 cm	12 in (1ft)

BEST SELLERS BY SNAB

Excellence in Books

101 Paneer Recipes

101 Vegetarian Recipes

SPECIAL Vegetarian Recipes

Cakes & Cake Decorations

Lebanese cooking for the Indian kitchen

101 International Recipes

Burgers & Sandwiches

Vegetarian MUGHLAI

CHOCOLATE Cookbook

Indian Vegetarian Favourites

BEST SELLERS BY SNAB

Excellence in Books

Pizza & Pasta

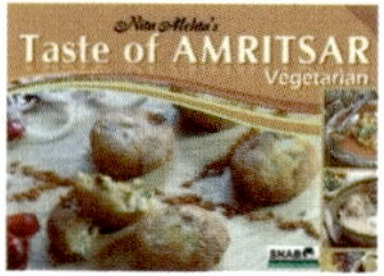

Taste of Amritsar (Veg)

Taste of Hyderabad (Veg)

Chinese Veg. Recipes

Soup & Salad

Breakfast Recipes

Paneer Recipes

Paranthas & Rice for Kids

Punjabi Recipes

Paranthas Aachars & Chutneys

Recipes for Growing Kids

Cooking Under 10 Minutes

CAKE cookbook

Tiffin Recipes for Children

INDIAN Vegetarian Recipes

Chatpati Chaat

Snacks & Chaat

Cakes & Cookies

Vegetarian Recipes

Zero Oil Recipes